Forgetting YOUR PAST

Forgetting YOUR PAST

Bob Gass

Bridge-Logos

Alachua, Florida 32615 USA

Bridge-Logos

Alachua, Florida 32615 USA

Forgetting Your Past

Copyright © 2000 by Bob Gass

Library of Congress Catalog Card Number: 2006932356

International Standard Book Number: 0-88270-817-1

Bible translations (abbreviations) used:
NIV   New International Version, Copyright © 1973,1978,1984 by the
International Bible Society. Used by permission of Zondervan Bible
Publishers.
TLB   The Living Bible, Copyright © 1971 by Tyndale House Publishers,
Wheaton, IL. Used by permission.
TM   The Message, Copyright © by Eugene H. Peterson, 1993,1994,1995.
Used by permission of NavPress Publishing Group
NAS   New American Standard, Copyright © 1960, 1962, 1963, 1968, 1971,
1972, 1973, 1975, 1977 by the Lockman Foundation Used by permission.
KJV   King James Version
CEV   Contemporary English Version, Copyright © 1995 by Thomas
Nelson. Used by permission.
AMP   Amplified Bible, OT Copyright © 1965, 1987 by The Zondervan
Corporation. The Amplified NT copyright © 1954, 1958, 1987 by the
Lockman Foundation. Used by permission.
NLT   New Living Translation. Copyright © 1999 by Tyndale House
Publishers. Used by permission.

Dedication

"A friend loveth at all times" (Proverbs 17:17).

My life took a dramatic turn for the better the day Mike Murdock entered it. I've thought a thousand times of the blessings I've derived from his friendship. Not a day goes by that I'm not enriched by the things he's deposited in me. And it's time I said so!

In the good times, our friends know us. In the bad times, we know our friends. To the Paulk family, I want to say, "Thank you" for always being there for me.

To Alex, Austin, and Caitlin—my grandchildren. Your presence is sheer joy.

May you be half as proud of me as I am of you. May you find in these pages the wisdom to be even better tomorrow than you are today, and may you always remember that my prayers will be with you wherever you go.

Table of Contents

Introduction

"Turn Thou me, and I shall be turned"
(Jeremiah 31:18).

Lord, I don't want to feel this way anymore. I thought that if my pain touched their lives, I'd feel better. I didn't. I thought that by holding it over their heads, I'd feel better. I didn't. I thought that by telling everyone what had been done to me, I'd feel better. I didn't; it only cost me friends and kept the pain alive longer. I thought if only they'd acknowledge how wrong they've been (and how right I've been), I'd feel better. They didn't, so I felt worse.

I thought if only I could understand why I picked such people, I'd feel better. So I read books and talked with counselors, but that didn't work, because I then discovered other things I didn't have the emotional energy to deal with. I thought time would make me feel better. It helped, but it didn't heal, because there were still too many things that triggered old memories. I thought that by moving someplace else, I'd feel better. I didn't. I only changed addresses, not what was going on inside of me.

Finally, I did two things, and they worked—not overnight, but gradually, patiently, consistently, as I kept doing them, they worked.

First, I decided to forgive—and keep on forgiving—until it didn't hurt anymore. Second, I cried out to God, "Turn Thou me, and I shall be turned."

He heard my cry! Suddenly my mind began to clear, and my emotions began to heal. Why? Because at last I'd reached the place where getting well meant more ... so much more to me ... than staying sick! Selah!

One

"... God HAS made me forget all my troubles"
(Genesis 41:50 NIV)

I had been molested twice by the time I was twelve. Once by a minister. My older brother Nei, experienced the same thing—yet we were both in our forties before we could even begin to talk to each other about it. Shame grows best in the dark; we're only as sick as the secrets we keep.

For me healing began when I could face it, forgive it, and deal with the shame I'd taken in as a result. Once I was able to do that, I could use it to help others.

In these pages, I'll share with you some lessons I learned that enabled me to close the door on my past, and move forward into the best days of my life. Here are four of them:

First, refuse to live like a victim! When I decided to stop looking for sympathy and start looking for solutions, I began to get well. God opens doors, but when He does, we've got to walk through them and accept responsibility for our future.

Second, isolate the problem. Everybody is not the same. I had to learn not to let what one or two people did to me infect every other relationship in my life. Once I was able to isolate the event, I could stop the enemy from using the past to rob me of the future.

Third, let "perfect love" heal your scars. I discovered that God's love for me was the only love perfect enough to cast out all my fears. (1 John 4:18) Fear of what? Fear of trusting others or myself! Fear of being known—and rejected! Only in the classroom of His love could I be set free from these fears.

Fourth, don't stop with God! His love and acceptance were the prescriptions that healed me—so that I could help make others whole too. You can only keep it, if you give it away. Listen: Joseph named his firstborn "Manassah" and said, "It is because God has made me forget all my trouble." The second son he named Ephraim and said, "It is because God has made me fruitful in the land of my suffering" (Genesis 41:51-52 NIV).

This book was written to help you do two things:

first, to learn how to forget your past, and second, to go on and become "fruitful" in every area of your life.

Two

Dealing with the Past

Every experience you've had from the moment you were born until now (and even while you were in your mother's womb) has made you what you are today. The things that happened to you, especially during your earliest years, determine how you'll act (and react) for the rest of your life.

That's what Jesus meant when He said, "A good man gives out good from the goodness stored in his heart; and a bad man gives out evil from his store of evil." (Matthew 12:35 Phillips) There are things stored up in each of us that must be dealt with before we can move ahead successfully.

Psychologists estimate that we spend up to 50 percent of our mental and emotional energy repressing painful memories.

My brother Neil, who spent many years in private practice as a Family Systems Therapist, tells me that the counseling community has recently done a one hundred and eighty-degree turn. Instead of saying, "Dig deep and go back as far as you can," they're now saying, "If the patient needs to vent, let him. But make it brief; then get him focused on the future as quickly as possible."

That's what some would call, "a sudden revelation of the obvious."

Two thousand years ago the apostle Paul wrote, "Forgetting those things which are behind, and reaching unto those things which are before …" Philippians 3:13). Paul understood that forgetting and reaching are the keys to inner healing. One will not work without the other. Forgetting closes the door on the past; reaching opens the door to the future.

You say, "What did Paul have to forget?" Plenty! On his orders, Stephen, the first Christian martyr, was stoned to death. Paul watched the whole gruesome scene. Could you forget that? Listen to his testimony: "… I persecuted the church of God, and wasted it" (Galatians 1:13 KJV).

"Wasted"—that's a Mafia term. While Christians slept, Saul of Tarsus and his zealots would break down their door, and, oblivious to the cries of children, take some parents to prison and others to the chopping block.

But now he goes back to those same towns to preach and when he stands in the pulpit, guess who's sitting in the pews? The widows! The orphans! If Paul had not learned how to deal with his own past, he never would have written one of the thirteen best sellers we now call "epistles" or founded a church that would last for two thousand years.

This, then, is the man who writes, "This one thing I do, forgetting …" (Philippians 3:13). This book is written especially for three people; you could be one of them.

Three

Those Who Cannot Forget What God Has Forgiven

The Bible is a book of forgiveness. In it God says over and over again that He'll forgive us. But not one of those promises is worth the paper it's written on unless we agree with him, and apply that forgiveness to our own lives.

You say, "But why wouldn't people be glad to hear and receive that?" For two reasons:

1) Because they don't "feel" forgiven, and therefore they conclude that they must not "be" forgiven.

This was the case with a young lady we'll call Julie, an attractive 20-year-old. As I sat looking at her across my desk I could see how difficult it was for her to talk about it.

Society calls it incest. For her it was a seven-year nightmare.

When she was only eleven, her father began to sexually molest her. For the next seven years she lived in a prison of shame, fear, false guilt, and confusion. It ended the night her father turned his life over to God, and asked her to forgive him. After that, the drinking and the daily outbursts of violent temper stopped. Her dad was a different man.

Yet, when they were alone or when he'd try to show his affection with a simple hug, she'd freeze. "I pull back," she said. "I can't help it. I hate myself when I see the hurt in his eyes. I know God has forgiven him, but I can't forget what he did to me." She broke. Sobbing, she buried her head in her hands.

She was living in a prison called "memory."

What is memory? It's that faculty that enables all of us to relive yesterday. That means you can be hurt every day of your life if you can't forget!

When Joseph said, "God has made me forget all my trouble" (Genesis 41:50 NIV), he wasn't talking about blocking out any remembrance of the jealousy, the hatred, or the abuse he'd experienced at the hands of his own brothers. No, that's denial! God's way, as the three Hebrew children discovered, is not out of the fire but through it.

How does God heal the wounds of our past?

He does it by anesthetizing the hurt, so that the memory is now surrounded by peace, not pain. Instead of a mausoleum to preserve what we can neither talk about nor get over, it becomes a monument to God's healing touch and a milestone on our journey toward wholeness.

2) The second reason that some of us can't forget what God has forgiven is that we have a wrong concept of God.

What is the God of your understanding like? Distant or personal? Loving or judgmental? Available or absent?

Every parent stands in the place of God until a child can know God for itself. Consider that for a moment. God is a provider, but from whose hand do we first receive? Our parents. God is a forgiver, but where do we get our first and most enduring concept of how forgiveness works? Our parents.

Now if you were raised by someone who said they forgave you, yet they kept "pulling your file" and constantly reminding you of your mistakes, you were probably given a distorted picture of God.

Each time you pray the words, "Our Father," what do you see? An angry God you can never please? An absent God who's not there when you need Him? An accusing God who never lets you forget anything you've done? How you related to your earthly parents will largely determine how you relate to your Heavenly Father.

Perhaps you need—a whole new concept of God!

If you do, listen to what God says about His love for you. "I have loved thee with an everlasting love: therefore, with loving kindness have I drawn thee." (Jeremiah 31:3)

Next, listen to what he says about His plans for you. "For I know the plans I have for you," says the Lord. "They are plans for good and not for evil, to give you a future and a hope" (Jeremiah 29:11 TLB).

Now listen to what he says about His forgiveness. "I, even I, am He that blotteth out thy transgressions for mine own sake, and will not remember thy sins" (Isaiah 43:25). Forget your sins for **God's** sake, for when you keep bringing them up, you bother Him with something awful!

In Old Testament days, when a man sinned, he brought a lamb to the altar to be sacrificed as payment for his sins. But please note: the priest didn't examine the man; he examined only the lamb. Why? Because if the lamb met all of God's requirements, then the man was automatically accepted and forgiven.

That's still how it works!

When you fail, all you need to do is approach God and say, "Father, I come in the name of Jesus." The moment you say that, the Father's focus moves from you to Him, and you're automatically accepted and forgiven. What an arrangement!

But you must also forgive yourself! If you don't, you're putting yourself above Him, and that's idolatry! If a perfect God, with full knowledge of your sins, says He'll forgive you, then on what grounds do you, an imperfect sinner, refuse to forgive yourself—or anybody else?

Perhaps you think you have to suffer a little first, to atone, at least in part, for what you've done—especially if it's in an area where you keep failing over and over again.

"You get nothing for nothing in this world," one man told me as he struggled to accept God's forgiveness. "For nothing?" I said. "Sir, the forgiveness you're being offered is the most precious thing in the universe! It may have cost you nothing, but don't ever forget—it cost God everything!"

It's pride that makes us think we've got to pay, at least in part, for what we've done. Yes, there are consequences for our actions, but don't make the mistake of thinking that those consequences are some form of atonement for your sin. No, if you have to pay one penny of your sin debt, that makes you a co-redeemer with Jesus Christ. Nothing insults the Cross more than that kind of thinking.

When Jesus cried, "It is finished," he wrote "Paid in full" across every sin debt you owed. No more will ever be required, and no less will ever be accepted.

Four

Those Who Cannot Forget What Someone Else Has Done to Them

"Why do you move so often?" I asked her.

She was in her mid-forties, the mother of four. We were sitting, talking in her doublewide trailer on the outskirts of town. Her husband was out in the back, tinkering with an old car. He never did come in and join us. I wondered why. They seemed like such a fine couple, and I'd dropped by to welcome them to our church.

When I asked, "How are you?" she suddenly dropped her head, apologized for her tears, and said, "The past ten years have been hell."

Then she told me her story.

She'd had an affair over a decade ago in one of the northern counties. Fighting to regain her composure, she said, "When I confessed to my husband what I'd done, he left me and the kids and stayed gone about a week. Then he came back and told me he'd forgiven me and that it was never to be mentioned again."

"I was so happy. I've tried every way I know to make up for it: to love him and be the best wife I can. But hardly a day goes by now that he doesn't bring it up. He's so bitter. He keeps saying, 'How could you do it to me?' But before I can answer, he'll storm out of the house. He's jealous of my having friends. He resents it if I even look happy."

"We've moved nine times in the last ten years."

When I asked her why, she replied, "I guess he's hoping we'll find someplace on earth where the past won't catch up with the present."

Has someone hurt you? Even betrayed you?

Have you ever noticed in the Bible that God doesn't 'whitewash' His heroes? Even though he was married, Abraham the patriarch lied and said he was single in order to save his own neck. (Genesis 20) And what about Samuel the prophet? For forty years he led the nation, yet he allowed his sons to run wild and bring disgrace to his family. (1 Samuel 8:5) And it's hard to think about the Apostle Peter without remembering how he denied His Lord. (Luke 23:54)

Yet these are the people God uses. Indeed, they are the only people He has to use—people just like you and me.

Some say, "Love is blind." Not God's love, that's 20/20. He knows the worst about us, yet He believes the best, for He sees us not just as we are, but as we will be when grace has done its work in us.

The reason we can't understand God's love is that we've nothing to compare it to. Nothing in our past or our present relationships qualifies us to understand such love—yet it's the greatest healing force on earth!

Five

Those Who Cannot Forget What They Have Done to Others

I saw this one day at a graveside committal.

The crowd had left and I was offering a word of condolence to the family when a big muscular man in his fifties suddenly leaned his head on my shoulder and sobbed, "Pastor, I never once told my father I loved him. We had words, but they were always angry words. So often I wanted to tell him how I really felt, but I couldn't. I was just too proud, and so was he. Now it's too late!"

Another time, I was 19 years of age and traveling in upper New York state as an evangelist. The service had ended in the tiny Italian church where I was preaching and a lady called me aside. "Do you think God will ever forgive me?"

The question took me by surprise. "Yes," I said. My mind raced, wondering what she could have done to bring on such guilt. "There's only one unpardonable sin. All the rest are pardonable, so I know God will forgive you." She continued, "Tonight when you told of committing your life to Christ as a boy of twelve and then starting to preach at thirteen, I thought my heart would break."

I realized this mother was probably opening up for the first time.

"My son is 21," she said. "He's already married and divorced and has been using drugs for the last eight years. But when he was twelve he came home from church one night and told me he had given his heart to the Lord. Back then I had no use for religion, so I just laughed at him.

"About a month later when he said he wanted to be baptized, I got so mad that I slapped him and told him never to go back to that church again. To my knowledge, he's never been inside a church since. Tonight he's in prison—and it's all my fault! Do you think God will ever forgive me?"

That night as we prayed, God enabled her to

accept His forgiveness—and to forgive herself! Peace filled her heart, and for the first time in years she was able to lay it down.

Did you know that when the ancient Persians found a man guilty of murder, they punished him by strapping the corpse of his victim to his back? What a picture! The weight of it dragged him down, the presence of it constantly tormented him, and the sight and smell of it drove others away. Eventually, it robbed him of his life.

That's the picture Paul had in mind when he wrote, "Who will rescue me from this body of death?" (Romans 7:24 NIV)

You can no more live with the dead things of your past clinging to you than Paul could! That's why you need the power of God to cut the cord between you and them. Whether it's past failure or past relationships, get rid of them. Don't walk around with them on your back or on your mind.

Nothing is heavier than bitterness.

Here's what it will do to you: 1) It'll drag you down and turn living into merely existing. 2) It'll cause you to leave a bad smell wherever you go. Even those who love you will become exhausted and leave, or confront you and say, "Get over it!" 3) It'll destroy every new relationship God wants to bring into your life. After all, who wants a person who's having an affair with a corpse? You'd only be using the new, as an anti-depressant to numb the pain of the old. 4) It'll destroy your health and shorten your life because you weren't built to carry it. Cut it loose! Cry if you need to, but when the grieving is over, bury it and move on.

You say, "I can't help but remember." Oh, yes you can! Paul said, "This one thing I do, forgetting those things which are behind ..." (Philippians 3:13)

Paul chose to forget. And so can you!

You say, "But it's so hard to do." Jesus didn't say all things are easy; He said all things are possible. (Mark 9:23) You'll do a lot of growing up between what's easy and what's possible!

Inherent in every promise God makes to you is the potential to see it fulfilled. Contained in every command He gives you is the power to carry it out. With that in mind, read the following promises and begin to personalize them.

"Fear not, for you will not be put to shame; neither feel humiliated, for you will not be disgraced. But you will forget the shame of your youth, and the reproach ... you will remember no more" (Isaiah 54:4 NAS).

"Do not call to mind the former things, or ponder the things of the past. [Note: don't recall them and don't dwell on them.] Behold I will do something new, now it will spring forth. Will you not be aware of it? [God has something new in mind for you; don't miss it!] I will even make a roadway in the wilderness [and] rivers in the dessert" (Isaiah 43:17-19 NAS, Author's notes added).

"The former things shall not be remembered or come into mind … be glad and rejoice forever in that which I create" (Isaiah 65:17-18 NAS).

Did you notice the word "create"? God can create order out of chaos and beauty out of ashes. He can help you to find purpose in the middle of your pain.

You may say, "Aren't those verses all from the Old Testament?" Yes, but listen: "He always does exactly what he says. He carries out and fulfills all God's promises no matter how many of them there are" (2 Corinthians 1:19-20 LB).

The one who said, "Behold I create new heavens and a new earth, and the former things shall not be remembered nor come into mind," stands ready to do two things for you: Create peace in the midst of your storm, and heal the painful memories that keep you chained to the past.

You may be down today, but you don't have to stay there!

Forgetting Your Past

Six

The Ladder

I want you to imagine the healing of memory as a ladder with seven rungs.

The moment you put your foot on the first one, you've already begun to rise above your past. If you wait until you "feel" like climbing, you'll never begin. Consult your will, not your emotions. Feelings should follow—not lead! What's called for here is "a quality decision" on your part.

It takes a smonly all act of courage to start, but a big daily dose of it to keep going, because you'll feel like quitting a thousand times before you get to the top.

Where does that kind of courage and tenacity come from? Three things: the books you read, the relationships you form, and the time you spend with God.

Listen, "Who, for the joy that was set before him, endured …" (Hebrews 12:2 KJV). What is it that enables you to endure painful struggles and rise above discouragement and setbacks? It's the joy of knowing that day by day you're getting closer to your goal. What goal? The goal of taking back your life and becoming what God wants you to be.

It's not easy. If it were, everybody would be doing it. But if you're sick and tired of being sick and tired, and you're ready to do something about it, then let's start climbing.

Seven

Rung 1: "Repent!"

Some people's idea of a good sermon is one that goes over their head and hits their neighbor right between the eyes.

Too many of us are like the man who walked into the psychiatrist's office with half of a melon on his head and a piece of bacon wrapped around each ear. The psychiatrist rubbed his hands with glee, thinking, "I've got a live one this time." Suddenly the man with the melon hat and the bacon ears sat down, looked at him, and said, "I've come to talk to you—about my brother!"

You may smile, but if you're not the problem, then what's the solution?

God's way is to tell it like it is! He doesn't put a bandage on an infected wound; He insists that it be lanced, drained, cleansed, and given time to heal.

King David took the wife of one of his own army officers, got her pregnant, and then had her husband killed to cover it up. What a mess! The child died, scandal rocked his throne, and civil war broke out. But worst of all, he permitted "… the enemies of the Lord … to … blaspheme …" (2 Samuel 12:14).

Finally he stopped running, stopped hiding, and got honest. Listen, "Then I let it all out; I said, I'll make a clean breast of my failures to God. Suddenly the pressure was gone—my guilt dissolved, my sin disappeared" (Psalm 32:5-6 TM).

I challenge you today to kneel down and do the same thing. Don't ask God to fix others—ask Him to fix you! Real healing can only begin when you let God take control of the thing that has had control of you.

If you think your past disqualifies you from moving forward, then you don't understand God's grace. He always has more for you today than you lost yesterday!

But you say, "I've had a child out of wedlock; I've been divorced; I've been in prison; I've had an abortion; I've violated the trust others placed in me;

I've lost so much." Don't be discouraged: God's not moved by our virtues; He's touched by "... the feeling of our infirmities." (Hebrews 4:15). Listen carefully to these words: "For since he himself has now been through suffering and temptation, he knows what it's like ... and he is wonderfully able to help us" (Hebrews 2:18 LB).

Can somebody with a past touch God in the present, and their future be forever changed? Yes! Yes! Yes! The hymn-writer wrote:

There is a fountain filled with blood,

Drawn from Emmanuel's veins;

And sinners plunge beneath that flood,

Lose all their guilty stains.

Case closed! Debt paid! Record expunged!

The rewards of repentance are awesome. Listen to Job: "Prepare your heart and lift up your hands to Him in prayer! Get rid of your sins, and leave all your iniquity behind you. Then your face will brighten in innocence. You will be strong and free of fear. You will forget your misery. It will all be gone like water under the bridge ... you will have courage because you will have hope. You will be protected and will rest in safety. You will lie down unafraid, and many will look to you for help" (Job 11:13-19 NLT).

Go ahead! Step into the river of God's mercy and let it flow over you, setting you free. Whether it's the guilt of something you've done, or the pain of something that was done to you, let it go—let it rush on by!

There's one more thing you need to know.

Repentance is not just "feeling sorry" for what you've done. It's a quality decision to break with the past and all its associations, pleasures, habits, and thought patterns. It's an about-face-turn.

When my son Neil was little, he had an aversion to soap and water; he hated getting washed. Every night bedtime was like a wrestling match. One night during the struggle, he looked up at me and said, "Dad, wait!" I could tell something good was coming. "Okay," I said. "What do you have in mind?" With a big grin he replied, "Couldn't you just dust me off a little?"

Repentance is not a light dusting; it's a thorough washing.

If you don't know how to repent, just read the words of David in Psalm 51 and make your prayer. Here they are:

"Have mercy on me, O God, according to your

unfailing love; according to your great compassion blot my transgressions. Wash away all my iniquity and cleanse me from my sin. For I know my transgressions, and my sin is always before me.

"Against you, you only, have I sinned and done what is evil in your sight ... cleanse me with hyssop, and I will be clean; wash me, and I will be whiter than snow ... create in me a pure heart, O God, and renew a steadfast spirit within me.

"Do not cast me from your presence or take your Holy Spirit from me. Restore to me the joy of your salvation" (Psalm 51:1-12 NIV).

That prayer changed David's life, and it'll change yours, too, if you pray it and mean it.

Eight

Rung 2: Receive God's Grace!

How does God put up with us? How can He keep forgiving us over and over again?

The answer is grace—nothing but grace! Paul said, "God, for Christ's sake hath forgiven you" (Ephesians 4:32). God forgives us the ten thousandth time for exactly the same reason He forgave us the first time—because of the Cross.

That's the only account any of us can draw on!

Because we live in a "performance based" society, we tend to approach God hoping we've earned enough credits to offset our debits. The trouble with that is, we keep failing and quickly reach the point where we feel like we've no credits left to draw on. Then we assume that God can't or won't forgive us—or that we'll have to work harder to obtain what He once offered us freely and willingly. How sad!

What we need here is a new pair of spiritual glasses to see God as He is and to understand how His grace works.

Shortly after my 50th birthday, my wife Debby suggested that I should get checked for eyeglasses. (I believe it had something to do with my driving!) I thought, "This is too much; first my hair, then my teeth, now my eyes."

Finally I gave in and went to see the optometrist.

You folks with glasses know the drill. The doctor put me in a chair, turned out the lights, and asked me to read several lines of black letters on a white background. At the top of the screen they were large; at the bottom they were small. So I decided I'd show the doctor and Debby and anybody else who cared that whatever Bob Gass may have needed, it wasn't glasses.

In my most fluent, well-modulated voice I read across the bottom line—"A.G.C.P.I.W.Z."

The doctor burst out laughing. I said, "What's so funny, doc? I just read the bottom line with the smallest letters and I never missed a one." She replied, "Reverend, I think we have a problem here; those are not letters—they're numbers—and you need glasses worse than anybody I've ever met!"

When it comes to understanding God's grace, most of us don't know the difference between letters and numbers. Listen, "Saving is all His idea ... it's God's gift from start to finish ... we neither make nor save ourselves ... God does both ..." (Ephesians 2:8-9 TM). Could language be any clearer?

Somewhere I heard about a Sunday school teacher who tried to explain the following verse to her students: "Ho, everyone that thirsteth, come ye to the waters, and he that hath no money, come ye, buy and eat; yea, come, buy wine and milk without money and without price" (Isaiah 55:1 KJV).

How do you explain such a verse to a class of six- or seven-year-olds?

The teacher decided to throw the question out to the kids, "What does it mean to buy without money?" After a long pause, one boy's hand shot up into the air and he said, "I know; my mother does it all the time. It means charge it!"

Forgiveness—yesterday, today and forever—is available to you through grace, but only on credit. His credit. Charge it to Jesus!

Upon a life I did not live
Upon a death I did not die
Another's life; Another's death;
I stake my whole eternity.

Nine

Rung 3: Make Restitution

The true basis of all inner healing rests in our willingness to forgive, and, when possible, to make amends to those we have hurt.

Zaccheus had to, and you do too!

Even though he was a Jew, Zaccheus worked for the system that enslaved his people; he collected taxes for the Romans. Now, tax collectors were among the most hated people in society because they usually extorted more than the system demanded, and got rich doing it. That's why everybody was so shocked when Jesus said to Zaccheus, "I must abide at thy house" (Luke 19:5).

One of the reasons that I love Jesus is because he

wasted no time being sanctimonious.

He allowed a prostitute called Mary to anoint His feet while the religious crowd whispered about His "spirituality." He took risks on people; aren't you glad?

He even used Rahab the harlot, then listed her in His royal family (Matthew 1:5). Now there's "a family secret" most of us would have shied away from revealing—but not Him. He tells us about this woman whose shameful reputation was cleansed by the blood—because He wants you to know that He can do the same for you, if you'll only come to Him today by faith.

God's grace is most clearly displayed in the lives of broken people.

Listen, "God is not ashamed to be called their God" (Hebrews 11:16). I'm glad He wasn't ashamed of Rahab, for that means He isn't ashamed of you and me either. If He could brag about Rahab's faith beside men like Moses and Joshua and Samuel, then who are we to condemn anybody?

What a wonderful thing it is to be adopted and acknowledged by God! He gives His name to the nameless, and removes the shame of the past. No wonder sinners loved Him. He, who had every right to throw stones, never threw one. How strange then that we, who have no right at all, are so quick to judge.

The Bible makes no mention of what Jesus said to Zaccheus over supper that night. But it must have been pretty powerful stuff, for as He listened, this con man cried out, "Lord, here and now I give half my possessions to the poor, and if I have cheated anybody out of anything, I will pay back four times the amount" (Luke 19:8 NIV). When Jesus heard his confession and his willingness to make amends, He said, "Today salvation has come to this house" (Luke 19:9).

Remember again, the true basis of all inner healing rests in our willingness to forgive, and when possible, to make amends to those we have hurt.

There is no "statute of limitations" in God's kingdom when it comes to responsibility. If you owe someone a debt, pay it! If you've hurt them, apologize and try to make restitution. Jesus said, "If you enter your place of worship and … you suddenly remember a grudge a friend has against you … leave immediately, go to this friend and make things right. Then, and only then, come back and work things out with God" (Matthew 5:23-24 TM).

That leaves no "wiggle-room" for any of us, does it?

Ten

Rung 4: Renounce It!

Shame ... fear ... rejection ... insecurity ... and resentment ... are all 'trespassers' in your life. They have no right to be there!

"So why do they persist?" you say.

Perhaps I can explain it this way. Each of us has a circle of perfect protection around us. But when we sin and refuse to deal with it, we break that circle and open ourselves to things like shame, fear, rejection, insecurity, and resentment. By refusing to repent, forgive, and make amends, we invite these things in and give them control.

Years ago when I visited Jim Bakker in prison in Rochester, Minnesota, he looked at me across the dining room table and said, "God has forgiven me for so much; but He has also let me know that I'll never get out of here until I forgive every person that ever hurt me."

I remember thinking, "That's motivation to forgive!"

Whether it's something you did or something that was done to you, the only way out of the prison of resentment is through the door of forgiveness. Listen again to the words of Jesus: "If you have anything against someone, forgive—only then will your heavenly Father be inclined to wipe your slate clean" (Mark 11:25 TM).

Few things affect me more deeply than that which touches one of my children. If you're a parent, you know what I mean.

Eleven years ago my daughter Kathy married a boy she'd met in the choir of one of Atlanta's largest churches. It was an exciting time. Our family gathered from around the world to celebrate the event and launch the happy couple on their way.

It lasted seven months!

The same day Kathy received her Master's Degree from Georgia State University, her new husband walked in, told her he was gay, and gave her a week to leave! Seven days later her bags were packed, and he was sharing their apartment with someone new—a man!

You say, "How did you feel?" When I saw my daughter curled up in a fetal position, broken and sobbing with uncontrollable grief, I wanted to kill him. Was I wrong to feel that way? Yes! But before I could change my feelings, I first had to own them and confront them—and that process took time.

The last thing I needed at that moment was some "Job's comforter" to come along and tell me I had "no faith," or that I was "acting immaturely."

Jesus said, "Blessed are they that mourn: for they shall be comforted" (Matthew 5:4). Not only is it healthy to express your emotions in the right way, it's self-destructive not to. When you try to 'stuff' them, they just drop from your conscious into your sub-conscious, and what you refuse to deal with then begins to deal with you!

Those undealt-with emotions will eventually begin to "break out" in other areas of your life in things like workaholism, over-eating, substance abuse, and other forms of compulsive or aberrant behavior.

Listen carefully to these words: "Happy are those who are strong in the Lord, who want above all else to follow your steps. When they walk through the valley of weeping, it will become a place of ... blessing and refreshment ... they will grow constantly in strength." (Psalm 84:5-7 TLB).

Did you hear that? You've got to walk through the place of weeping to get to the place of blessing. There is no other way!

I knew that by holding the sword of condemnation over the head of my former son-in-law, I was not only disobeying God, but also keeping the pain alive longer in me.

As I prayed about it, I began to realize that David had married my daughter hoping that she could "fix" him, or help him to go "straight." Once I began to understand that, my anger turned to compassion and I was able to pray for him. That was my first step toward being able to forgive him.

Did I feel like it? No! Was it easy? No! But if I was going to help Kathy and keep bitterness from growing in my life, then I had to forgive and move on.

Each day and many times throughout the day, I'd pray, "Father, by an act of my will, I freely forgive David as You have forgiven me. And whatever I ask for myself in blessing, I ask for him in double measure. Amen."

At what point, or after which particular prayer

did my feelings change?

I don't know! But I can tell you this: I had to make a decision to forgive—and keep on forgiving—until it lost all the power it had over me. I also had to keep moving forward, because if I'd lingered too long in the valley of weeping, I'd never have gotten out of it.

Eleven years have passed, and Kathy's now married to a great guy called Michael Shea (an Irishman of note). Recently they made me the happiest man in Georgia by presenting me with my first granddaughter, Caitlin—"The Princess!"

As I mentioned before, some of the things from which we need to be set free are so deeply rooted in us that they've moved from our conscious to our sub-conscious. We suffer their effects, yet we don't understand their cause. That's why we need God to bring them to the surface and help us to deal with them one by one.

Once we've identified the problem, we must be willing to repent of our part, forgive others of their part, and accept complete forgiveness on God's part.

To get free and stay free, sometimes we must break the enemy's hold and renounce his work in our lives. This is done simply by using the Name of Jesus.

Here's how it works: the mention of that name

brings to the Father's attention the finished work of Calvary through which all our victories are won and all our needs are met. But the ultimate force in using the name of Jesus is in repeating it in the ears of Satan, our defeated foe, and insisting on his retreat. As you pray using that name, he must go—reluctantly—angrily—he MUST loosen his clutches and retreat!

No matter what you're battling with today, you can say with authority, "I come against you in the Name and through the Blood of Jesus, and I break your hold over my life." Those are powerful words because His name gives you the authority to say it, and His Blood gives you the assurance that it has already been paid for and provided.

Jesus said, "I tell you this; whatever you prohibit on earth is prohibited in heaven ..." (Matthew 18:18 NLT). The one thing the enemy doesn't want you to know is that you have the power to restrict his movements in your life. You're a child of God. You carry your Father's "power of attorney," so put the handcuffs on and serve him an eviction notice.

At this point, I have a word of warning for you; don't take it back!

A lie is as good as the truth—if you believe it! If you were a millionaire, and I could convince you that you were penniless, you'd live in want and die in need. Why? Because you believed what I told you! The thoughts that chain you to the past are a lie. Don't believe them! Go back to God's Word and find out what He says about you, for that's what will set you free (John 8:32).

At this point, let's take a moment and deal with three of the enemy's strategies.

The first is feelings. Through your reason he tells you, "You don't deserve to be free." Through your emotions he tells you, "You don't feel like you're free." Here is where victory is decided. Stand your ground. The work is done in you. God's Word says so. Now you must begin now to say so too. Time will strengthen and solidify your position.

Since the devil doesn't give up territory without a fight, expect to be tested on this. If you don't, you'll be caught off guard. Time and time again he'll come back and offer you the same old issues all wrapped up in the skin of reason and emotion.

Remember, it's only skin—not substance.

Don't vacillate or be "double-minded," for that creates paralyzing indecision—the inability to act victoriously or to walk in your newfound freedom. Paul said, "This **one** thing I do, forgetting …"

(Philippians 3:13) He was characterized by single-mindedness. You must be too!

Satan's counter-attack then is this; first, he brings back to your mind the things God has set you free from. By having to deal with them again, you'll experience many of the same emotions you had when you were actually bound by them. That's the way he plans it. The idea is to make you feel like nothing has changed. Don't buy it!

His second strategy is shock. If you're not expecting to be attacked, you'll think, "I must not be making any progress at all, or else why would I still be fighting the same old battles?"

His third strategy is to get you to speak negatively. He wants you to say things like, "What's the use? Nothing's changed!" When you begin to speak like that, you're signing the receipt and accepting the package. Don't do it! The Bible says, "You are snared with the words of your lips, you are caught in the speech of your mouth" (Proverbs 6:2 AMP). Guard your words, for they create the atmosphere you live in. Never say things that make the enemy think he's winning.

But you say, "How can I live victoriously over these things? " By taking these four steps:

1) Soak yourself in the Scriptures.

Jesus said, "Man shall not live by bread alone, but by every word which proceedeth out of the mouth of God" (Matthew 4:4). Three times the tempter tried to get Jesus to submit to his suggestions, but each time He responded, "It is written …" After the third attempt, Satan left Him alone because he can get nowhere with the man or woman who knows the Word of God and stands on it.

When the enemy tries to plant his thoughts and suggestions in your mind, have your "It is written" ready. Build yourself up on the Word of God—before the attack comes.

The Greek root for "word" is sperma. Think about that! God's Word is His very life and seed! It's creative; as you read it, remember it, and repeat it. It will reproduce in you what it says. Therefore the secret of victory is to initiate your response to every attack—from the Word which you have hidden in your heart.

2) Develop the habit of prayer.

The enemy knows what your potential is, and he's out to stop you before you get there. Prayer puts a shield of divine protection over you! Don't live without it!

There are people reading this book who thought that they, of all people, would never cheat on their taxes or their partner, but they did. Look out! Unless you acknowledge the propensity for sin that's within you, you won't pray against it, and you'll always be vulnerable at that point.

Jesus said, "Stay alert; be in prayer so you don't wander into temptation without even knowing you're in danger. There is a part of you that is eager, ready for anything in God. But there's another part that's as lazy as an old dog sleeping by the fire" (Matthew 26:41 TM). Could language be clearer?

The most effective weapon the enemy has against you is—you! That's why your old nature must be taken daily to the cross and crucified. The place of prayer is where you do that! As you spend time in God's presence, you see yourself as He sees you, and there at the point of repentance, He begins to reveal, remove, and restore.

You say, "Restore what?" Your peace of mind, the respect of your loved ones, the courage to dream again, the ability to love and be loved in a healthy way, and the strength to say, "No" to every destructive force that's ever ruled your life.

Every 50th year in Israel, God declared A Year of Jubilee. When the trumpet sounded that year, three things happened for God's people: every prisoner was set free; every debt was cancelled; and everything that had been taken from you had to be restored.

Think about that! God can break every chain that links you to the past; He can wipe the slate clean of every mistake you've ever made; He can restore everything that's been taken from you—if you'll just seek Him and serve Him.

3) Burn your bridges.

Any bridge to the past that you refuse to burn just gives the enemy an invitation and an entry point back into your life.

Israel discovered that if you're serious about going to the "Promised Land, you've got to leave Egypt—including the things you liked about it. More than once they wanted to go back to the way things were. Why? Because there's a certain security in staying with what you know and certain fearfulness in moving out into what you don't know.

Consider this: you'll give up a lot if you decide to move forward, but you'll give up even more if you stay where you are.

Once, when His disciples had fished all night and caught nothing, Jesus said to them, "Launch out into the deep" (Luke 5:4). What a challenge. The deep is where the great catches are enjoyed—and the great storms are experienced. You can't have one without the other. Stay in the shallows or launch out into the deep; the choice is still yours.

It's not easy to break with the past. The new Christians in Ephesus brought out all their old books of witchcraft and pornography and burned them in the town square. (Acts 19:19) When they did, a riot broke out. Sound extreme? Paul says, "Make no provision for the flesh, to fulfill the lusts thereof." (Romans 13:14) Be ruthless with yourself. If you give your flesh an inch, it'll take a mile.

Remember, change is inevitable, but growth is optional; you'll either fight it for flow with it, but know this—if you're not willing to leave Egypt, you'll never get to the Promised Land.

Author Gayle Sheehey says, "If you can't change, you won't grow, and if you're not growing, you're not really living. Growth means giving up familiar but limiting patterns, safe but unrewarding work, values no longer believed in, and relationships that have lost their meaning. Taking a new step or uttering a new word is what we fear most, but in reality, our fear should be the exact opposite."

Rabbi Samuel Silver writes, "The greatest of all miracles is that we need not be tomorrow what we are today, if only we'll use the potential implanted within us by God." I can't think of anything worse than living a stagnant life devoid of change and improvement—can you?

4) Learn how to rest and replenish your strength.

Blessed with success, but cursed with ambition, we self-destruct because we don't know how to take care of ourselves.

Samson could handle the might of a thousand soldiers single-handedly, but he couldn't handle the loneliness of an empty room, so he finished up in Delilah's lap. T. D. Jakes says, "Delilah's weapons were not her lips, hips and fingertips, but rather his tiredness, his numbness, and his inner void." What insight!

The Psalmist cried, "Thou hast been a shelter for me" (Psalm 61:3). David found his answer in God's presence! Samson never did, and it killed him! Delilah's lap looked so good that he stayed too long, talked too much, and lost everything.

When you're tired, you're vulnerable.

I know! I built a successful church and became a familiar face on two hundred television stations across America, but before it was over I "crashed and burned." I learned painfully that "He maketh me to lie down" (Psalm 23:2). He had to, because I didn't know how!

Your "Delilah" can be anything that comes into your life to deplete your strength. It can be a career, a relationship, or a habit. It's what you turn to when you need escape. Don't be fooled—she may delight you tonight, but she'll destroy you tomorrow. Get up while you can and run—don't walk—run to the arms of Jesus.

Isaiah says, "He gives strength to the weary, and to him who lacks might He increases power. Though youths grow weary and tired, and vigorous young men stumble badly, yet those who wait for the Lord will gain new strength; they will mount up with wings like eagles, they will run and not get tired, they will walk and not become weary" (Isaiah 40:29-31 NAS).

Rung 4: Renounce It!

Eleven

Rung 5: Rejoice!

"**N**o matter what happens, always be thankful."
(1 Thessalonians 5:18 NLT)

Introversion is a dangerous preoccupation with yourself. It always leads to depression and negativity. Why? Because inevitably you focus on what's wrong in your life instead of what's good.

Let me ask you a question. Have you ever met a perfectionist who was truly happy? I haven't!

Whenever things must always be a certain way, life can be pretty miserable, because life constantly changes. Instead of being content and grateful for their blessings, perfectionists constantly dwell on what's wrong and their need to fix it.

It could be a disorganized closet, a dent in their car, a job they did that was less than perfect, or a few pounds they'd like to lose. Or it could be someone else's imperfections, the way they look, the way they behave, or the way they live their lives.

The very fact that perfectionists constantly think about such things makes it impossible for them to be thankful—and an attitude of gratitude is basic to all happiness.

We're not talking here about striving for excellence; no, we're talking about fixating on what's wrong. Sure, there'll always be a better way to do something. But that doesn't mean you can't enjoy life the way it is at the moment.

Paul was in one of Europe's worst prisons when he wrote, "Rejoice in the Lord always. I will say it again: Rejoice!" (Philippians 4:4 NIV). That's what's called "an attitude of gratitude" and you've got to have it if you're going to survive and overcome.

Look at this man; they could lock him up, but they couldn't keep him down. Why? Because his perspective constantly lifted him above circumstances. Listen to him, "And we know that in all things God works for the good of those who love him, who have been called according to his purpose" (Romans 8:28 NIV).

When you're in the center of your God-given purpose, you can smile in the storm because you know—you absolutely know—you're coming out on top.

David said, "Seven times a day will I praise thee" (Psalm 119:164). Forget the coffee breaks; start having praise breaks! Punctuate your day with them because praise gets your eyes off the problem and onto the problem-solver. It changes your focus from what's wrong to what's possible.

"I will lift up my hands in thy name" (Psalm 63:4).

I noticed that when my grandchildren were learning to walk, they'd keep lifting up their hands. Then I discovered why. It was to give themselves a sense of balance. What a lesson! Your life will never be balanced if all you do is ask, but never adore—petition, but never praise.

If you want to come into God's presence, the Bible tells you to enter His gates with thanksgiving, cross His courtyard with praise and you'll find Him there waiting for you (Psalm 100:4).

When Alex or Austin or Caitlin would come toddling toward me with their hands up, I couldn't resist them. Even if they didn't look or smell too good, just one glimpse of those little faces and outstretched hands, and I was compelled to pick them up and hold them close.

And it's the same with your Heavenly Father!

When you reach up to Him and say, "I love You, I need you," He picks you up and carries you through the rough places. He holds you close to Himself and whispers, "Fear not ... thou art Mine" (Isaiah 43:1).

If you want potatoes, you'll find the best in Idaho or Maine. But if you want bananas, you'll have to go to Jamaica. Why? Because climate determines what can grow.

What's the point? Simply this: the strength that you need to overcome and the attitudes you need to keep moving forward can only be cultivated in a climate of gratitude and continual thanksgiving. In that kind of environment your faith will grow, your focus will change, and your memories will begin to heal.

When that happens, the power of the past will be broken.

Twelve

Rung 6: Repeat What God Says About You

I grew up around some people who could focus like a laser beam on—what's wrong. A thousand good things could pass them by without comment, but when a problem arose, they came to life. They were "experts" in such subjects as—why things are not the way they should be, why nothing ever changes, why nobody cares, and why things are not as good as they used to be.

Vance Havner tells of a lady, who once wrote to a newspaper editor and complained, "Your paper is not as good as it use to be!" He wrote back and said, "It never has been."

Words are powerful things; they either build you up or tear you down. They literally create a ceiling above which your faith cannot rise. That's why it's so important to line your words up with God's words.

To walk in victory you must begin to say what God says, regardless of the situation in which you find yourself. To say anything different is to put yourself in disagreement with Him. When you do that, you "pull the plug" on your own potential, and short-circuit the very power that works on your behalf.

You are what God says you are! If others disagree, so what? When you've got God's opinion, what difference does anybody else's make?

The only solid and enduring foundation for self-worth is God's opinion of you. And you'll find that in His Word. When you do, build your life around it and fill your conversation with it. Whether you're struggling or soaring, stand on the Word of God.

I challenge you to try reading the following words and not get excited:

"So, what do you think? With God on our side like this, how can we lose? If God didn't hesitate to put everything on the line for us ... by sending His own Son, is there anything else He wouldn't gladly and freely do for us?

"And who would dare tangle with God by messing with one of God's chosen? Who would dare to even point a finger? The one who died for us—who was raised to life for us!—is in the presence of God at this very moment sticking up for us.

"Do you think anyone is going to be able to drive a wedge between us and Christ's love for us? There's no way! Not trouble, not hard times, not hatred, not hunger, not homelessness, not bullying threats, not back-stabbing ... not even the worst sins listed in scripture ... none of this fazes us because Jesus loves us.

"I'm absolutely convinced that nothing— nothing living or dead, angelic or demonic, today or tomorrow, high or low, thinkable or unthinkable, absolutely nothing can get between us and God's love" (Romans 8:31-39 TM).

You wouldn't be so critical of yourself or so conscious of the opinions of others if you really knew how God felt about you! He made up His mind about you before you ever sinned. So repent and dismiss the guilt, for guilt is the offspring of unbelief. All it does is insult God's mercy.

Stop running from place to place, looking for love and security. Just open your heart; God's speaking to you today in the very circumstances you're trying to escape. He's the one you need when life has wounded you and you've fallen from your nesting place like a bird. Only His hand can catch your falling soul, cast it to the wind, and give you the strength to fly again.

Listen to what God says about you: "I have seen his ways, but I will heal him; I will lead him and restore comfort to him" (Isaiah 57:8 NAS).

The problem is, we've never been loved by anyone the way God loves us, so we've nothing to compare it to. Some of us have never been secure in the love of our natural parents, so we haven't learned how to relate to our Heavenly Father. Go back to His Word and see what He has to say about you. The Bible is a living love letter; it's a statement of intent from a God who wants nothing but the best for you.

But you say, "I fall so far short."

Nothing you've done has changed His mind about you, and nothing ever will. His love remains—it's unconditional. David said, "Your faithful love, Oh, Lord, endures forever" (Psalm 138:8 NLT). It has no cutoff point!

Bill Reilly heads up a ministry called Overcomers at the Cathedral of the Holy Spirit in Atlanta. In the last ten years he's worked with more than 15,000 people struggling to recover from various addictions and lifelong dysfunctions.

I remember once asking him, "What's the difference between those who make it and those who don't?" He replied, "The real overcomers are the ones who build their lives on the Word of God and practice its principles in all their affairs."

That just about sums it all up, doesn't it?

Thirteen

Rung 7: Restoration

"And I will restore to you ... the years ..."
(Joel 2:25)

Good news! You can start your life over again any day you chose. The past ended last night at midnight. Today is the first day of the rest of your life. Listen to this promise: "I will restore unto you ... the years ... (Joel 2:25). God says, "I'll give you new opportunities, new relationships, and a new beginning.

It's not too late for you. He's hiring in the eleventh hour.

Read the story Jesus told in Matthew, chapter 20, and you'll understand how God does things in His kingdom. You'll also notice how different it is to the way we do things.

In that story some workers were hired in the third hour, others in the sixth hour, others in the ninth hour—and some in the eleventh hour. This last group had only one hour left when the owner of the vineyard found them standing idle. The day was almost over, and they had nothing to show for it. Looking back, it must all have seemed like such a waste.

Their lives had no meaning and no value—until he came!

What a scene! First he redeemed them; then he recruited them to work for him. Even though they'd only an hour left, he took what they had and gave them back more than they ever dreamed possible.

The quotas were filled, the deadlines were met, and the work of hours was rolled into minutes. Then they all lined up to receive their wages.

To the consternation of some and the amazement of all, he gives those who were called in the eleventh hour the same wages as all the others. The first three groups complained that it wasn't fair. But he said to them, "I will give unto this last even as unto thee" (Matthew 20:14).

Fantastic! Only He can do that!

Look carefully what he told them. "Friend, I am not being unfair to you. Didn't you agree to work for a denarius? Take your pay and go. I want to give the man who was hired last the same as I gave you. Don't I have the right to do what I want with my own money? Or are you envious because I am generous?" (Matthew 20:13-15 NIV). What a question!

If you fall, not everybody will be generous enough in spirit to rejoice when you get back up!

Some weren't too pleased when the Prodigal Son came back home, especially his older brother. And there are still lots of "older brothers" around today. They'll point an accusing finger, but they'll never extend a helping hand. That's because they're more comfortable with your failure than they are with your success. How sad. They want what you've got, but they don't want to pay what you paid. They feel like your gain is their loss; that somehow your blessing came at their expense. Some of them may even feel like they have a right to blow your light out in order to let their own light shine.

Be discerning; there are basically three types of people: the users, the cautious, and the committed.

The users will reach for your strengths, but carefully avoid your weaknesses. When trouble hits your life, they'll distance themselves "in a heartbeat," lest they become tainted by your perceived liabilities.

Don't be resentful toward them. They're not bad, they're just weak and self-serving.

The cautious are a majority. When you're in trouble, they'll wait to see if you get out of it; and even then they'll "keep their options open." Before they reconnect with you, they'll first check and see who else does. Paul says, "… Know them which labor among you" (1 Thessalonians 5:12). When it comes to the cautious, love them, but don't build your life on them!

The committed are those Solomon talks about in Proverbs 17:17, "A friend loveth at all times and a brother is born for adversity." Remember the old adage, "In the good times our friends know us; in the bad times, we know our friends." If you have even a handful of committed friends, you're doubly blessed, for they'll stand by you "at all times." They're not just strong in faith, they're also strong in fight; they're "born for adversity." Protect those relationships. Nurture them, for without them you can't reach your God-given destiny.

One of the most famous Rose Bowl games in history was played on January 1, 1929, between Georgia Tech and the University of California. Near the end of the second quarter, a California linebacker by the name of Roy Riegels picked up a fumble, dropped his head, and raced toward the goal line. Fifty thousand fans went wild as he crossed it. When he looked up, he suddenly realized that half the stadium was hissing and booing, while the other half was roaring with applause.

It was a wide-eyed nightmare. He had run to the wrong goal line and he scored against his own team! Shocked and sickened, he dropped the ball and raced from the field in tears.

Now it's a painful thing to "blow it" at anytime, but when you do it at the Rose Bowl with the whole world watching—where can you go?

The following day every major newspaper carried the story, complete with action pictures. But the leading newspaper in St. Louis told a different story. It was the story of a magnificent second half-played by the same man. His blocking was crisp; his tackles were vicious; his throwing was pinpoint accurate.

The man who wrote this story was so in awe that he looked up the linebacker and asked him, "What made the difference?"

While the reporter scratched in his notepad, Riegels told him, "When I left the field that day, I was convinced I'd never play ball again. I was through! The team came in at halftime and I hid behind the lockers.

I was humiliated. I didn't want to talk to anybody—not even my own family—least of all, them. I even thought of suicide.

"When halftime ended, the coach called the lineup for the second half, and that's when I heard my name—'RIEGELS!' I couldn't believe it. I listened again, as the coach's voice boomed through the locker room—'RIEGELS!' I stepped out from behind the lockers and said, 'Coach, I can't go out there again. I can't face them.'

"I'll never forget what my coach, Clarence Pierce, told me that day: He said, 'Son, you made a mistake. It was a big mistake. But the game's only half over, and you're still on my team. I need you now more than ever, so I want you to go out there and give me the best you've got.'"

Looking hard at the reporter, this man who would ultimately become one of history's great linebackers said, "When I realized that my coach still believed in me, I could do nothing less than give him my best."

I don't care how many times you've fumbled the ball or run in the wrong direction, your coach still believes in you. He can give you victory in the last half, the last quarter, or even in the last moments of the game.

But you say, "I've fallen so often." Everybody falls. The winners are just the ones who get back up again! God wants you to know that you're still on the team, and that until the clock runs out, you can still be a winner.

The Bible says, "The word of the Lord came the second time unto Jonah (Jonah 3:1). He's the God of second chances—and third ones if you need them. Jonah, the runaway prophet, was corrected, cleansed, and called again—this time he got the job done.

When Jesus rose from the dead, He sent word to His disciples that he wanted to meet them in Galilee, yet the only one He singled out by name was Peter (Mark 16:17). Why? Because Peter's failure was so public and his despair so deep that without a personal invitation, he may have been lost forever.

In forty years of ministry I've never met a pulpit committee that would even consider calling Peter to be their pastor. Have you? Yet God made him the leader of the New Testament Church. (Too many gifted and valuable people have been lost to the Church, because we didn't know how to handle them.)

Only when you accept your failure as final are you finally a failure—but not until then.

John Maxwell says, "Failing doesn't mean I'm

a failure; it just means I have not yet succeeded. It doesn't mean I've accomplished nothing; it just means I've learned something. It doesn't mean I've been a fool; it just means I've had the courage to take a risk. It doesn't mean I'm inferior; it just means I'm not perfect. It doesn't mean I've wasted my time; it just means I have a reason to start over. It doesn't mean I should give up; it just means I must try harder. It doesn't mean I'll never make it; it just means I need more practice. It doesn't mean God has abandoned me; it just means He has a better idea!"

Fourteen

The Battle Is Your Future

"And about the fourth watch of the night [the darkest hour] he cometh unto them walking upon the sea" (Mark 6:48).

It was the worst storm the disciples had ever been in. They'd fought the wind and waves until there was no more fight left in them. Fear had them by the throats, and they were convinced that they weren't going to make it.

Have you ever been there? I have!

No matter how hard you try or who's right and who's wrong, when a marriage falls apart, two people feel like one giant failure. If you've ever been through it, you know what I'm talking about. If you haven't, I pray you never will.

Some of the harshest critics are mellowed when it comes knocking on their door or the door of someone they love. And it's all the more humbling when your claim to fame has always been, "We've never had divorce in this family."

I know. I used to say it!

I also know why God says that He "hates divorce." It's hell! There's no pain like it. When someone you've shared your life with, and would even have given your life for, turns around and rips you apart, it's hell. When friends say thoughtless things that only add insult to injury, it's hell. When children and loved ones are caught in a war of words because it hurts too much not to talk, it's hell. When loneliness is so real that it sucks every ounce of oxygen out of the room and peels the paint off the walls, it's hell. When you feel like you have to offer an explanation to everyone you meet because you're not sure what they've heard, it's hell.

Guilt is a healthy reaction, but shame is toxic; it can actually kill you.

Shame says, "You didn't just fail, you're a failure! You didn't just make a mistake, your whole life is a mistake! You're so flawed that you'll never be whole again and nobody will ever want you!" Such thoughts are just more lies from "the father of lies," but until you discover that, and deal with it, it's hell!

For me, the worst part was fear. I could imagine every door to the future slamming shut. I could also remember preaching to others, "If it doesn't work at home, don't export it!" Audiences loved it; now it all sounded so glib and ill considered.

One of the toughest things I had to deal with was the fact that my circumstances had changed, but not my calling. That remained the same. The Bible says, "God's gifts and His call are irrevocable" (Romans 11:29 NIV).

For me, the answer to pain was purpose!

Today when I talk to people who are lonely or depressed, I tell them, "Find a cause greater than yourself and pour life into it." I believe that's what Jesus meant when He said, "Except a corn of wheat fall into the ground and die, it abideth alone [it will always be lonely], but if it die [die to self: self-seeking, self-serving, and self-centered living] it brings forth much fruit [it will never be lonely again]" (John 12:24,

Author's notes included).

Loneliness is not the absence of affection; it's the absence of direction. My friend Tommy Barnett tells people, "If you want to get God's attention, find a need that nobody's meeting and give your life to it; that'll get His attention every time."

Looking back more than a decade later, I realize that while I made lots of mistakes, God gave me the wisdom to make some good choices too.

One of those choices was to reach for "a fathering spirit." Paul says, "Ye have ten thousand instructors in Christ, yet have ye not many fathers" (1 Corinthians 4:5). Think about that for a moment. A real father has the kind of love and maturity needed to keep you from making bad decisions about your future at a time when you probably shouldn't be making decisions at all. He'll also confront you about the areas in your life that must be changed; otherwise your past will just become your future.

But the real reason you need "a fathering spirit" is that only a father will love you unconditionally and do what it takes to get you back on your feet again. Why? Because he's committed to the purpose of God that must be fulfilled through you! If your life fell apart tomorrow, would you know where to find such a person?

Another good choice I made was giving myself sufficient time to be strengthened and made whole. When a crisis hits our lives, our first thought is usually "survival." We want to keep up appearances and stay alive economically. And that's understandable. But what good is it if you look healthy in public, while you're hemorrhaging to death in private?

If you find yourself in the place of personal devastation, or if someone you love is there today, here are some insights that helped me greatly from my friend Mike Murdock:

(1) Don't panic! Your biggest mistakes will usually happen during the first period of any crisis. Surprise is the enemy's strategy. If you're under attack today, listen: "Be still, and know that I am God" (Psalm 46:10). That means He's present, He's in charge, and He has a solution! Stop and listen carefully to the inner voice of His Spirit (John 16:13). Time is your friend. Patience is the weapon that always forces deception to the surface. Give God a chance to work on your behalf.

(2) Analyze it! Solomon said, "In the day of prosperity be joyful, but in the day of adversity consider ..." (Ecclesiastes 7:14). A crisis is merely

concentrated information. Take the time to analyze it, and you'll benefit from it.

(3) Seek worthy counsel! Listen, "Where no counsel is, the people fall" (Proverbs 11:15). Ignorance can be deadly. Don't risk it! Somebody knows something you need to know—something that can help you survive and even succeed in the most painful chapter of your life. Reach for them!

(4) Expect God to move! Listen, "When the enemy shall come in like a flood, the spirit of the Lord shall lift up a standard against him" (Isaiah 59:19). Adversity is just the enemy's reaction to your progress. Rejoice! The eyes of your Father are upon you.

(5) Guard your mind! You'll never be defeated as long as you're victorious in your mind; that's the birthplace for everything you do. Satan knows that, and he'll try to get your mind so scattered that you won't be able to concentrate on what's important. Don't let him. The Bible says, "Thou wilt keep him in perfect peace, whose mind is stayed on thee" (Isaiah 26:3). Get back into focus!

(6) Realize that you're not unique. Listen, "Be strong in your faith. Remember that your Christian brothers … are going through the same kind of suffering you are" (1 Peter 5:9 NLT). The devil would

love to convince you that you are the only person that's ever experienced anything like this. Why? So that you'll feel like a failure and quit, or cut yourself off from the support that comes from fellowship with others. Don't let him do it to you.

(7) Remove any hindrances! Listen, "Dear friends, if our hearts do not condemn us we have confidence before God" (1 John 3:21 NIV). We all sin; the mistake is trying to cover it up for, "He that covers his sins will not prosper" (Proverbs 28:13). If you're constantly being defeated, ask God to show you where the trouble spot is, and deal with it immediately.

(8) Fight back! You'll be tempted to withdraw or become timid and passive; especially if you've been hurt. Don't! A wounded animal only attracts attack. Satan loves shy, fearful types, but real fighters intimidate him. Be bold. "Resist the devil and he will flee from you" (James 4:7).

(9) See the big picture! Nothing is ever as it first appears. Look beyond the moment; something great is being birthed in you. After adversity comes blessing and favor, so get your eyes back on the big picture. Paul says, "This short time of distress will result in God's richest blessing" (2 Corinthians 4:17 TLB).

(10) Never, never, never give up! Jesus said, "No

one who puts his hand to the plough and looks back is fit for service in God's kingdom" (Luke 9:62 NIV). Your dreams and goals are worth … any fight … any price … and any waiting period. Your perseverance is what demoralizes the enemy. Remember Joseph? Every day of adversity was simply a stepping stone toward the throne. So keep walking and keep believing for victory!

For me the turn-around came at two o'clock one morning when the telephone rang in my apartment and it was Mike. He said that God had put me on his heart, and that he was calling to ask me two questions.

The first was, "When did Moses become a champion?" I replied, "When he was eighty." That's when he began to lead the children of Israel out of Egypt. The second was, "When did the enemy try to destroy him?" I replied, "When he was two." That's when Pharaoh ordered the death of every Hebrew baby boy in an attempt to get him.

The words that he spoke next changed my life.

He said, "Bob, hell plans eighty years in advance to destroy a champion and wipe out a winner. The battle is not over your past! The battle is not even over your present! The battle is over your future!"

In that moment light pierced the darkness,

depression lifted, and something inside of me rose up and declared, "Then I will live and not die, and I will declare the works of the Lord" (Psalm 118:17 paraphrased).

Ten thousand blessings have flooded my life since the night I first heard those words.

If you are reading this page, then those words are for you, too; the battle is over your future! The level of the attack only reveals your potential!

"But," you say, "I'm afraid I'll never be the same again." You're right. You can be even better—if you want to! In spite of his chapter of denial, Peter was. In spite of his chapter of defection, Jonah was. In spite of his chapter of degradation, David was. And you will be too! It's not too late for you. God says He'll restore to you the years which the enemy has stolen.

The only place the past can live is in your memory. The only power it can have over you is the power you give it.

Solomon says, "A just man falleth seven times, and riseth up again" (Proverbs 24:16). Bob Hoover is one of America's greatest test pilots. He's wrestled out-of-control jets back to the ground, fought fires in midair, and crashed many times. In one crash he broke his back and almost died. But as soon as he recovered, he climbed back into the cockpit of another Super Sabre and soared back into the heavens. When he was asked why, he responded in his Tennessee drawl, "Ya gotta get back into the cockpit of the bird that bit ya."

Hoover knows that any fear you won't confront will ultimately control you, and what you fail to conquer will rule your life.

Whether you crash in a plane, go bankrupt, or find your marriage or career on the rocks, you have to make the same choice: either allow the circumstances to destroy you or "get back into the cockpit of the bird that bit ya" and start over again!

Winners are just losers who got tired of losing; they decided to get up one more time than they were knocked down. The Bible is full of their stories. And by God's grace, you can get back up too. Listen. "The steps of the godly are directed by the Lord ... though they stumble, they will not fall, [stay down] for the Lord holds them by His hand" (Psalm 37:23-24 NLT).

Be like the man who said, "I'm never down, I'm either up or I'm getting up!"

The other day while watching Christian television, I noticed some very gifted servants of God who had walked through the fires of divorce and came out the other side with a new anointing, a new compassion,

The Battle Is Your Future

and a new mandate to touch hurting people. It's the broken who become masters at mending!

Some would have removed these men and women from the game and set them on the sidelines, in a well-meaning attempt to keep our standards high and our image clean. What a loss that would have been to God's kingdom! What a message that would have sent to a broken world!

Can we not also be lifted, healed, and restored by the same grace we preach to others?

What is our message? That you can be a major drug dealer like Nicky Cruz, or a mass murderer like the apostle Paul, and God will forgive you and use you. But if your marriage fails, you're disqualified for service in God's kingdom?

Let's get real!

People listen to our one-sided testimonies of success without failure and become discouraged. They think that while they struggle, we "have it all together" because we've falsified the records and failed to tell the whole truth. God help us! Our message is we were saved by grace, we are being saved by grace, and we will be saved by grace!

It was after David failed that mercy rewrote his life and enabled him to produce his greatest psalms—the

85

ones in which we all take comfort. It was because Paul filled jails (and graves) with believers that he cried, "I owe a great debt" (Romans 1:14 TLB), and then went on to spend the rest of his life paying it off.

Don't quit because someone's discovered that you're "a treasure in an earthen vessel." (2 Corinthians 4:7) There's a cry from the Jericho road that nobody but you can hear. Some dying thief will listen and be saved if only you'll keep preaching through your pain—for the message that saves others is the same one that saves us too.

Accepting the rejected is not the weakness of the gospel; it is its strength! There's a world of difference between the coldness of a rebellious heart and the cry of a troubled heart that says, "God, save me from myself!" One glimpse of God's grace brings all of us crashing to the floor on bended knees, confessing and forsaking sin, and "bringing into captivity every thought to the obedience of Christ" (2 Corinthians 10:5).

Before God covered Adam's nakedness, He first had to strip him of his façade!

That's our greatest concern—isn't it? We think, "If others really knew me!" Now, it's one thing to play that game with people who are similarly afflicted, but to play it with God is ridiculous.

You can be stripped before God, admit your mistakes, and still maintain your position as His child and as His servant. Indeed, it's only when you let God see you as you are that His grace (and his discipline) can begin to change you into what you need to be. (Hebrews 12:6)

When we strip away the layers, we're not so different, are we? The liar is as lost as the adulterer. Their symptoms may be different, but their cure is the same—"the sacrificed blood of Jesus, God's Son, purges all our sin" (Hebrews 9:22 TM).

T.D. Jakes says, "To the survivors of wrecked ships and damaged homes, we hold out our arms. As we do, they will come—the halt, the lame, the deaf, and the dumb. They will need much of the Word before their marriages cease to tremble and their self-images improve. They will have flashbacks and relapses, and require intensive care. Yet, we swing wide the door of ministry and admit that most of our doctors have at one time been patients, and that many of them are still being treated. But we say, 'Come,' for we are not the medicine—Christ is! To the overlooked and the castaway we cry, 'Come!' If nowhere else, and by no one else, you are accepted in the Beloved!" (Ephesians 1:6)

Forgetting Your Past

Fifteen

For the Next 21 Days

At this point I'd like to give you twenty-one daily readings; they're like capsules of truth. Take one each day. They'll nourish the seed that's been planted in you and help you develop a root system strong enough to withstand the storms in the days ahead. And storms will come!

Be patient with yourself! Recovery is not a hundred-yard dash, it's a marathon; not a giant leap, just a series of small steps. The first requires courage; the rest just require stick-to-it-ive-ness.

Remember, something else too: we do not determine our futures; our habits do. It's not what we do once or twice that makes the difference— it's what we do daily.

Each day for the next twenty-one days, I want you to find a place where you can be alone with God—and your thoughts. All you need is about ten minutes. If you have to drive to a quiet spot, or go for a walk, or lock yourself in the bathroom, do it. You're worth it!

Read each day at least twice. You'll be amazed what you'll get the second time, that you didn't even see the first time. If something jumps off the page or speaks to you personally, underline it. It's your book; you can do what you like with it.

When you're through reading, take a few moments and pray about what you've read. Don't be religious, just talk to God like you would to a loving Father or a trusted friend, for He's both.

And whatever you do, don't try to handle all your character defects at once or you'll get overwhelmed and quit. Just deal with one thing at a time, as God reveals it to you.

And don't worry about whether you can or can't do it. The truth is, by yourself you can't! God ordained it that way so that you'd learn to lean more on Him. Listen, "Trust in the Lord with all thine heart, and lean not unto thine own understanding" (Proverbs 3:5). This is called "forced dependence," and the independent streak in each of us hates it.

Paul actually referred to this as his "thorn in the flesh." Listen to how he describes it: "Three different times I begged the Lord to take it away. Each time He said, 'My gracious favor is all you need. My power works best in your weakness.' So now I'm glad to boast about my weakness, so that the power of Christ may work through me" (2 Corinthians 12:8-9 NLT).

How do you run a race? One step at a time. How do you live successfully? One day at a time. If you're ready to start running and start living again, then let's go!

Day One

"He healeth the broken in heart, and bindeth up
their wounds" (Psalm147:3).

Starting Again

Are you trying to recover from a broken
relationship? If so, don't rush into another one. Take
your time; unhealthy people make unhealthy choices.
Some wounds take longer to heal than others, but you
can count on one thing: "… he healeth the broken in
heart, and bindeth up their wounds" (Psalm 147:3).
Give Him a chance.

Begin by taking time to search His Word and
find out how He feels about you. His Word is the
only reliable basis upon which you can build your
self-worth. If a perfect God can love and accept you
with full knowledge of all your imperfections, then

the message is—"Lighten up on yourself!"

You can love and be loved again, but only with the same wholeness with which you love yourself (Matthew 22:39). Next time make sure your choices are healthy ones, not predicated on need or the fear of being alone.

And be careful; when you don't value yourself, you tend to attract people who do the same, including those who seek to control you or belittle you. You deserve better, so hold out for it. Remember, you train others to treat you by how you treat yourself.

As you become healthier, you'll start to see how unhealthy some of your choices have been. If some people walk away say, "So be it." Sometimes you've got to give up less, if you want God to give you more.

God's got wonderful relationships in store for you, but He's waiting until your values and your perceptions line up with His. So take it step-by-step, one day at a time. And don't forget to rejoice, for your **best** days are still ahead of you.

Day Two

"He will give you all you need from day to day if you live for Him and make the Kingdom of God your primary concern" (Matthew 6:33 NLT).

Alone—and Thriving!

As you begin to discover how God feels about you, your memories will heal, your self-worth will be restored, and you'll stop trading with a devalued self-image.

Get rid of the idea that anybody's company is preferable to your own. In a recent survey of thousands of "happy" couples, 52 percent confided that they wouldn't marry the same person again! Think about that, and you'll realize the answer to loneliness is not people—it's purpose!

John was alone on an island when God revealed to him the glories of heaven. Paul was alone in prison when he wrote the epistles. God did His best work when He was alone with no one to applaud Him, so He praised Himself, saying, "It is very good!" (Genesis 1:31) Can you do that?

When others say nice things about you, it reflects their opinion of you, but when you can speak well of yourself, it reflects your opinion of yourself—and that's the one you live with every day.

Somewhere beyond loneliness there's a contentment that's born of necessity. It's when your options close in the natural that doors start to swing open in the spiritual. That's when you begin to see the possibility of having the kind of relationship with God that you've never had before. Think about it.

Day Three

"I press on ..." (Philippians 3:14 NAS).

Press On

When "the bottom falls out" what do you do? Blame others? That only makes you bitter. Wallow in self-pity? That only paralyzes you and alienates others! When David returned from battle and found his home burned to the ground and his family taken prisoner, he cried until he had no tears left.

But then we read, "David strengthened himself in the Lord his God" (1 Samuel 30:6 NAS). That's it! You've got to learn how to get alone and give yourself a good talking to! You've got to learn how to pray for yourself and to quote God's promises to yourself! Here's one: "Weeping may endure for a night, but joy cometh in the morning" (Psalm 30:5). Did you hear that? "Joy cometh!" Change is on the way!

Learn how to rise up and say, "What does not destroy me will only make me stronger! No day lasts forever. This too shall pass. In the meantime, it will only drive me closer to God." Come on, start talking to yourself!

Your weakness can be the discovery point for strengths you never even knew you had! When Joseph recalled the worst time of his life, he said, "God turned into good what you meant for evil" (Genesis 50:20 TLB).

Others don't control your destiny—God does and he's not like others! You will come out of this stronger and wiser! Look beyond the pain and you'll find perspective. The word for you today is: regroup, renew and reload—and whatever you do, keep pressing on!

Day Four

"We should make plans, counting on God
to direct us" (Proverbs 16:9 TLB).

Take Control of YOUR LIFE

You can change your life any day you want to.
Here are some steps you can take today.

1.   Discern what success really is. When others
feel good about you, you're popular! But when you
feel good about yourself, you're successful! If you
don't know what you're supposed to do, here's a
clue: your life's highest purpose will always create the
highest level of joy within you. That doesn't mean it'll
be easy or pain-free. Every winner in the Bible paid a
price and you will too.

2.   Prayerfully set goals. Success is achieving the
goals God has for you. It's not wrong to make plans,

it's just wrong to worry about the future. Solomon said, "We should make plans counting on God to direct us" (Proverbs 16:9 LB). What are your goals? How do you plan to reach them? Do you pray about them regularly?

3. Stop looking for somebody else to bring you happiness. Don't wait for flowers to arrive; God gave you seed, start growing your own. Listen, "… Let every man prove his own work … then he shall have rejoicing in himself alone, and not in another" (Galatians 6:4). When you're less "needy," you'll actually become more attractive.

4. Get over the past. We all have a past— some are just "better advertised" than others. A friend of mine was praying one day: "Father, why does the devil keep reminding me over and over about my past?" God replied, "Because he's running low on material!" What a great answer! God says that He will not remember your sins (Isaiah 43:25). That means that unless you're wiser than He is, do the same thing—and get on with your life!

Day Five

"... No good thing he withold from them that walk uprightly" (Psalm 84:11).

When God Says, "No!"

If it were a good thing, God would not have said, No. Either the timing is wrong or He has something better in mind for you. The real issue here is—do you trust Him?

Gratitude comes when you realize what could have happened, but didn't because God intervened on your behalf. So stop trying to break loose from the loving grip of the One who holds you for your own protection. Just submit; God knows what's best for you!

David said, "The Lord is my shepherd" (Psalm 23:1). Think about that. A shepherd is just someone who leads, feeds, and protects his sheep. What a picture—God watching over you! He's like a lifeguard at the beach; to save you, he'll interrupt the festivities, risk embarrassing you in front of your friends, and maybe even bruise a rib or two. That's because He loves you too much to let you drown in the very thing you think is "so good for you."

Billy Graham's wife Ruth says, "If God had said 'yes' to all my prayer requests, I'd have married the wrong man—several times." Sound familiar? Listen, "Commit thy way unto the Lord; trust also in Him; and He shall bring it to pass" (Psalm 37:5). What you're bitter about today, you'll bless God for tomorrow.

Mark Twain said that when he was fourteen, his father was so ignorant he couldn't stand to have him around. But by the time he was twenty-one, he was amazed how much the old man had learned in seven years. The more you mature, the more you'll begin to see how loving and wise your Father is.

Day Six

"Grow in grace and understanding"
(2 Peter 3:18 TM).

Developing the Right Attitude

Toward Yourself

Here are ten principles to help you develop and maintain a healthy self-image. Read them slowly. Meditate on them regularly.

1) Hate your sin, but never hate yourself.

2) Be quick to repent.

3) When God gives you light, walk in it.

4) Stop saying negative things about yourself. God loves you as you are, and it's wrong to hate what He loves. He has great plans for you, therefore you're in conflict with Him when you speak negatively about

your future.

5) Never be afraid to admit that you've made a mistake, but don't always assume that when things go wrong, it must be your fault.

6) Don't meditate excessively what you've done, right or wrong; both of these activities keep your mind on you! Center your thoughts on Christ. Listen, "You will guard him and keep him in perfect and constant peace whose mind [both its inclination and its character] is stayed on you" (Isaiah 26:3, AMP.).

7) Take good care of yourself physically. Make the best of what God gave you to work with, but don't be obsessed with your appearance.

8) Never stop learning; but don't allow your education to become a point of pride. God doesn't just use you because of what's in your head; He also uses you because of what's in your heart.

9) Realize that your talents are gifst, not things you've manufactured yourself, and never look down on people who can't do what you do.

10) Don't despise your weaknesses; they keep you dependent on God.

Day Seven

"It is God Himself who has made us
what we are" (Ephesians 2:10 TLB).

Rejoice in Who You Are

Avoid relationships with people who don't value themselves, for they won't value you either. Look for those people who enhance you, not inhibit you; look for those who fertilize your mind and put the wind beneath your wings. When you're around people like that, you'll see your best qualities through their eyes and grow from the wisdom that falls from their lips.

When you encounter somebody who tries to tell you that you've nothing to offer, be sure to laugh. It's impolite to hear a joke and not laugh. When God made you He said, "… It was very good …" (Genesis 1:31). That's God's opinion of you, so why give anybody else's the time of day? You're full of such potential that the word "possibility" is written all over you. By God's grace you can be anything He desires you to be—and that's true whether you're eighteen or eighty-eight!

If you're regretting your past, remember, God's looking at your future. His love for you isn't based on your performance or your virtues. Listen, "But God commendeth His love toward us, in that, while we were yet sinners, Christ died for us" (Romans 5:8). God loves you "Calvary-worth" That's the value God places on you, and that's how you should begin to see yourself.

Listen to Paul, "There has never been the slightest doubt in my mind that the God who started this great work in you would keep at it and bring it to a flourishing finish ..." (Philippians 1:6 TM). Rejoice, He's brought you this far, and He'll take you the rest of the way. That's a promise!

Day Eight

"If anything is excellent or praiseworth—think about such things" (Philippians 4:8 NIV).

Change How You Think

You don't have more problems than other people—you just think about them more often!

It's what you think that produces how you feel. If you don't believe that, try getting angry without first having angry thoughts, or sad without having sad thoughts. You can't do it! To experience a feeling, you must first have the thought that produces it!

So what can you do? Change how you think and you'll change how you feel! Nothing can hold your negative feelings in place other than your own thinking. The next time you're feeling upset, notice your thinking—it'll be negative. It's always that way.

The truth is, it's your **thinking** that's negative, **not your life**! Once you understand that, you're back on the path toward happiness again.

But change takes time; you didn't become negative overnight and you won't become positive overnight. But you can start. You say, "How?" By treating your negative thoughts in the same way you'd treat flies at a picnic—shoo them away and then replace them with thoughts that are "excellent or praiseworthy."

Day Nine

"It matters very little to me what you think of me
... the Master makes that judgement"
(1 Corinthians 4:3-4 TM).

Free From the Opinions of People

If you let it, criticism will ... steal your individuality ... rob you of your creativity ... and stop you from fulfilling your destiny. Insecure people will always criticize you; specially if your choices are different from theirs. Why? Because they're uncomfortable with things that don't conform to their way of thinking.

On the other hand, secure people can handle being the only one doing something. They can allow others the liberty to be different and to make their own choices, because they're secure in who God has called them to be.

Listen, "He made himself of no reputation" (Philippians 2:7). Jesus obviously wasn't too concerned about what others thought of Him. He had a goal—to do the Father's will—no more and no less. He also knew that to do it, He had to be free from the opinions of others! So do you!

The greatest tragedy that could happen to you would be to grow old and know that somewhere along the way you'd lost yourself, and never succeeded at being who God called you to be. Don't let that happen! Paul says it this way: "It matters very little what you think of me, even less where I rank in popular opinion. I don't even rank myself … the master makes that judgment" (1 Corinthians 4:3-4 TM). Today ask God to help you become free from the opinions of others. _

Day Ten

"As the Spirit of the Lord works within us, we
become more and more like Him"
(2 Corinthians 3:18 TLB).

The Need for Change

Did you hear about the frog that fell into a big
hole and couldn't get out? Several of his friends tried
to help, but finally they gave up. "Since you're going
to be in there for a while," they said, "we'll go and get
you some food."

But no sooner had they left than the frog came
hopping up behind them. "We thought you couldn't
get out!" they exclaimed. "Oh, I couldn't," he replied.
"But suddenly there was a big truck coming right at
me—and I discovered that I could!"

Usually it's only when we're forced to change,

that we discover we can! That's because we're more comfortable with old problems than new solutions.

If you believe nothing should ever be done for the first time, then you'll never see anything done, and nothing will change.

There are three times in our lives when we're most receptive to change. First, when we're forced to. Second, when what we're doing no longer works. Third, when we realize that we can change! Nothing sparks the fires of desire more than the sudden realization that "I don't have to stay this way anymore!"

Be encouraged today: God is at work in your life, changing you bit by bit—as you lean on Him.

Day Eleven

"Whoever accepts anyone I send, accepts Me" (John 13:20 NIV).

Can You Receive from Others?

You'd be surprised how many of us live beyond help—because we have an image to uphold. That's a dangerous place to be! When trials come, not only must you be open to the Lord, but also to whoever He chooses to send your way.

Listen, "And he was in the wilderness forty days, tempted of satan; and the angels ministered unto him" (Mark 1:13). Even Jesus needed the strength that comes from others. After forty days of fasting, He was hungry, and Satan offered to satisfy that hunger in a perverted way: "Command these stones to be made bread" (Matthew 4:3). One of the hardest things to do is say "no" when you have a legitimate need that you could satisfy in an illegitimate way!

Even though He created the angels, He permitted them to minister to Him. The greater was willing to receive help from the lesser—what a lesson for us!

When your pain level gets high enough, you won't care who God uses! If you were in a burning house, you wouldn't care who the firefighters were, would you? Their education, their denomination, or their ethnic backgrounds would mean nothing to you because of the urgency of your need.

Perhaps your problem is that you need someone, but you don't trust anyone. Start trusting God! Who do you think brought you this far? Listen: "Though the mountains be shaken and the hills be removed, yet My unfailing love for you will not be shaken, nor My covenant of peace be removed, says the Lord who has compassion on you" (Isaiah 54:10). When God extends His love and compassion to you, don't be too proud to accept it in whatever form it comes! For when you do, you're accepting Him.

Day Twelve

"Be on the alert … Stand firm in the faith …
Act like men … Be strong"
(1 Corinthians 16:13 NAS).

Toughen Up!

Where did you ever get the idea that everybody would appreciate you? Certainly not from Jesus! He said His blessings were reserved for the "persecuted and the reviled" (Matthew 5:10-11). If you are 'thin skinned,' you'll have a rough time, because that makes you an easy target for the enemy.

Endurance is the secret, not popularity! Paul endured … desertion by his friends … ugly letters from the Corinthians … disappointment with the Galatians … mistreatment in Philippi … mocking in Athens … plus imprisonment and beheading in Rome.

(And you're complaining?) He writes four things to which you need to pay careful attention today:

(1) Be on the alert! Why? Because you have an adversary who is out to get you. What's he after? The deposit of God that's within you. You are a seed capable of producing a harvest for God in the earth.

(2) Stand firm in the faith! Why? Because you can't stand on your feelings, your circumstances, or the opinions of others. Those things change constantly. You can stand only on the Word of God.

(3) Act like men! Why? Because being childish won't cut it when the battle rages. It's time to grow up! If you're still making the same mistakes twenty-five years later, you're not learning enough.

(4) Be strong! Why? Because weakness is an invitation to your enemy. Furthermore, it always precedes surrender, and quitting is not an option for you. God told His people that the Promised Land was theirs, but they had to fight for it, and God's saying the same thing to you today!

Day Thirteen

"The word is near you; it is in your mouth and
in your heart, that is the word of faith"
(Romans 10:8 NIV).

Faith Talk

Your tongue is one of the greatest gifts God has
placed at your command. Use it wisely! The Bible
says, "Life and death are in the power of the tongue"
(Proverbs 18:21). Strong words—yet so often we don't
stop and think before we speak or consider the effect
our words will have.

Have you ever used words like, "I can't handle
this" or, "This will never change?" I know I have!
Your words don't just affect those around you—they
affect God. Faith-talk is what He responds to. What
you say about your situation affects what you believe,

and what you believe determines what you'll receive from Him.

Are you talking about your expectations, or are you still rehearsing past experiences? Listen, "Out of the same mouth come praise and cursing. My brothers, this should not be" (James 3:10 NIV). It's so easy to slip from speaking faith into speaking fear.

Make a decision today to guard your words carefully. And remember—others may not speak words of faith to you today, so practice speaking them to yourself.

(By Debby Gass)

Day Fourteen

"Beloved, think it not strange concerning the fiery trial which is to try you" (1 Peter 4:12).

The Refiner's Fire

It takes fire to purify gold, and when God gets ready to refine us, He uses fiery trials. Nothing brings luster to your character and commitment to your heart like adversity. Whenever you see someone whose life reflects the character of Christ—you're looking at somebody who's been through the fire.

Is that where you are today? If so, rejoice, for God has His hand on the thermostat! He knows the temperature required to burn away the things that hinder His purposes in your life. His hand fans the flames needed to teach you patience, prayer, forgiveness, faith, and a lot of other character-building lessons. You need His correction—you don't enjoy it—but you need it.

Listen, "All discipline for the moment seems not to be joyful, but sorrowful, yet to those who have been trained by it, afterwards it yields the peaceable fruit of righteousness" (Hebrews 12:11 NAS).

No one invests without expecting a return, and God is a wise businessman. He'll do whatever it takes to protect His investment in you.

We spend so much of our time talking about what we want from God, when the real issue is what He wants from us—and what He'll do to get it. John said, "He'll place everything true in its proper place … everything false He'll put out with the trash to be burned" (Matthew 3:12 TM). Perhaps that will help you to understand better some of the things that are happening in your life at the moment. Think about it!

Day Fifteen

"Behold, I will do a new thing; now it shall spring forth" (Isaiah 43:18).

Are You Ready?

If God says He's going to bless you, then disregard the circumstances and believe the God who cannot lie! The rubbish can be cleared and the bruises can be healed. Just be sure that when the smoke clears, you're still standing! You are too important to God to be destroyed by a situation that was meant to give you character and direction.

Think about it; you survived—by the grace of God you made it! God has proven that He can bring you out of the fire without even the smell of smoke, and out of the lions' den without so much as a bite mark!

If you want to know what God can do, just look

at what He's already done—and you'll start feeling better about your future.

And that's not all. Listen, "Behold, I will do a new thing; now it shall spring forth." After feeling like you've waited forever, God will move suddenly and if you're not ready, you'll miss the open door, the great idea, or the new relationship He has for you. Be alert; live in expectation!

When the Church was born, we read, "Suddenly there came a sound from heaven" (Acts 2:2). When God miraculously brought Paul and Silas out of prison, we read, "Suddenly there was a great earthquake … and immediately all the doors were opened" (Acts 16:26). Are you ready for God to move suddenly?

Day Sixteen

" Come ye yourselves apart ... and rest a while"
(Mark 6:31).

Take Some Time Out!

If the light on your inner dashboard is flashing red, you're probably ... carrying too much ... too far ... too fast. If you don't pull over, you'll be sorry. But if you've the courage to call "time out" and start making some changes, you'll be well rewarded.

But be warned; there are three problems you'll face the moment you do.

First, you'll experience "false guilt." By saying "no" to the people to whom you've always said "yes," you'll feel a twinge of guilt. Ignore it—it's false guilt! It's based on wrong thinking and screwed-up values. Retune your conscience to God's Word and the priorities of His Kingdom.

123

Second, you'll encounter hostility. Certain people won't understand your slower pace and your new priorities, especially those who are still in the sinking boat you just stepped out of. Stick to your guns. In time, those who matter most will see the wisdom of what you're doing. Hey, they may even follow you!

Third, you'll get some painful insights. By not filling every spare moment with activity, you'll begin to see the real you—and you may not like some of what you see. Business can be a great place to hide. But if you begin to deal with things as God brings them to your attention, you'll turn the corner and be well on the road to a healthier, happier, freer, and more fulfilling life.

Your goal should be to fulfill your destiny, and in the process to stay … in balance … in good health … and in God's will! Think about it!

Day Seventeen

"The Lord corrects and disciplines everyone whom
He loves" (Hebrews 12:6 AMP).

Can You Accept His Correction?

You say you want to change? Well, real change
can't even begin until you first believe that God loves
you as you are; otherwise you'll just keep trying to
change yourself in a vain attempt to earn His love and
approval. The problem with that is, you already have
it—you just don't know it!

Most of us are afraid that if we accept ourselves
as we are, we're excusing what's wrong in us. Not
so! You can't receive God's correction properly until
you have a revelation of His love for you. Otherwise
you'll see His disapproval of your actions only as
disapproval of you.

To grow up spiritually, you must first believe that God is committed to you, for often He'll deal with you correctively, and lead you in ways you don't understand. During those times, you must have a firm grip on His love for you! The Apostle Paul was convinced that **nothing** could ever separate Him from God's love (Romans 8:38-39). Are you convinced of that?

Listen, "Those whom I [dearly and tenderly] love … I tell their faults, and convict and convince … reprove and chasten" (Revelation 3:19 AMP).

The strongest evidence of God's love **and approval** of you is the fact that He convicts you and corrects you. If you're going through that process right now, rejoice; it means He has some wonderful things in store for you!

Day Eighteen

"A man must be content to receive the gift
which is given him from Heaven"
(John 3:27 AMP).

Just Be Yourself!

Has it dawned on you how much "they" control your life? How often have you said, "Well, you know what they say?" "They" set the standard and we wear it ... drive it ... or do it!

Now that may be Okay in some areas, but not when it comes to your life's direction. Jesus said, "If the son liberates you [makes you free men], then you are really and unquestionably free" (John 8:36 AMP). That means you're free from the pressures others try to put on you ... free to be who God has called you to be ... and free to look to Him for your own answers instead of always running to other people.

Listen, "A man must be content to receive the gift which is given him from heaven" (John 3:27 AMP). Think about that! Because of my background I really struggled with insecurity. I was competitive. I kept comparing myself with others. I was jealous of their possessions, their abilities, and their accomplishments. I was always trying to keep up with certain people— or be like them!

As a result, I was constantly frustrated because I was operating outside of what God had called me to be. In other words, I wasn't being myself!

When I finally realized that I could only be what God had ordained me to be, I rose up and began to say, "I am what I am. I can't be anything other than what God has called me to be. So I'm just going to concentrate on being **the best me** that I can be." You need to say that too!

Day Nineteen

"Be strong and courageous ... For the Lord your God goes with you; He will never leave you nor forsake you" (Deuteronomy 31:6 NIV).

Go ahead, take the risk!

Take a good look at what's left of your life and decide to make it count! Start living! General MacArthur said, "Whatever your years, there is in every heart ... the love of wonder ... the undaunted challenge of events ... the unfailing child-like appetite for what comes next. You are as young as your hope, and as old as your despair."

It's frightening for all of us to take risks and try new things. We think, "What if I fail?" What if you do? It won't be your first mistake, and no matter how bad it is, it won't be your worst mistake, and unless you fail at something really big like attempting to climb Mt. Everest or swim the English Channel, it won't be your last mistake.

The one thing you can count on is, whichever way it goes, you'll gain in wisdom, experience, and character. In other words, you'll become a better person for just having tried.

Refuse to listen to those who've settled for second best and want you to do the same. Your goal is not to live long—it's to live now! At 100, Abraham became a father, at ninety Caleb claimed a mountain, and at seventy Paul went to preach in Rome. Go Ahead! Do whatever God puts into your heart. What good is your life if you don't live it?

Day Twenty

"… God, Who Tests Our Hearts"
(1 Thessalonians 2:4 NIV).

Are You Passing the Test?

Why does God test us? Why does anybody test anything? (1) To observe it under pressure. (2) To see if it's reliable. (3) To reveal its flaws and correct them. (4) To develop it to its full potential.

When God tests you, it's to see if he can trust you. You mean he doesn't know? Sure he knows – but unless you know and acknowledge your weaknesses, you won't submit to his corrective hand. (Hebrews 12:11). Furthermore, when he sends people to help you, you'll rationalize and resist.

What you've been taught is worthless until it's first been tested! Each time you pray, "God, use me," you're inviting Him to take you to the next level. That means being stretched!

The test you're going through right now is just an indication of the level of blessing that's waiting for you on the other side of it! Why did God test Abraham by asking him to sacrifice his son Isaac? (Genesis 22) Because of what He planned to do through him. God was saying, "If you pass this test, I'll make you: (a) the father of many nations, (b) the standard by which faith is measured, (c) an example to the world of what it means to walk in my blessings."

Listen, "Remember how the Lord your God led you all the way in the desert these 40 years, to humble you and test you, in order to know what was in your heart" (Deuteronomy 8:2 NIV). The word for you today is—move closer, lean harder, stand strong, for when this test is over, God has great things in store for you.

Day Twenty-One

"I tell you, now is the time"
(2 Corinthians 6:2 NIV).

Every Day is Special

These words by Anne Wells should make you sit up and think! "My brother-in-law opened the bottom drawer of my sister's bureau and lifted out a package. In it was an exquisite silk slip, with the price tag still attached. Jan had bought it the first time she went to New York, about 8 or 9 years ago. She never wore it; she said she was saving it for a special occasion. Well, I guess this is the occasion.

"He put the slip on the bed with the other clothes we were taking—to the funeral home. Suddenly he slammed the drawer shut, turned to me and said, 'Don't ever save anything for a special occasion. Every day you live is a special occasion!'

"Those words changed my life; I'm not saving anything anymore. Now we use our good china and crystal for every special occasion—like losing a pound, getting the sink unstopped, or the first camellia blossom. 'Some day' and 'one of these days' are losing their grip on my vocabulary. If it's worth seeing, hearing, or doing, I want to do it now! I'm trying very hard not to put off, hold back, or save anything that would add laughter or luster to our lives. Every morning when I open my eyes, I tell myself—today is special."

Makes you think, doesn't it? Makes you want to drain the last ounce of joy out of every day and break free from the concrete of procrastination that whispers, "You can do it later." Wise-up; forgive that offense! Tell that person you love them! Take that trip! Go back to school! Decide now to do the thing you've been putting off, for today is that special day you've been waiting for.

Acknowledgments

The Finishing Touch, Charles R. Swindoll (Word)

Don't Sweat the Small Stuff, Richard Carlson, Phd. (Hyperion)

How to Succeed at Being Yourself, Joyce Meyer (Harrison House)

Can You Stand to Be Blessed, T. D. Jakes (Treasure House)

Seeds of Wisdom, Dr. Mike Murdock (Wisdom International Inc.)